THE JEWISH BOOK OF IF

Questions for the Jewish Game of Life

Rabbi Schachar Orenstein

with Karin Tulchinsky-Cohen

Cover designed by Eva Ifrah

Rabbi Schachar Orenstein
Visit my website at www.rabbischachar.com

Printed in the United States of America

First Printing: March 2019
Dharma Den Publishing

ISBN-978-0-9921411-0-3

"There is a world of 'if' which you can enter if you dare for the benefit of your soul. This book is a gate."

Rabbi Zalman Schachter-Shalomi
Co-author of *Jewish With Feeling*

"The Jewish tradition insists that it is in our hands to make our own destiny. This book will help you make yours. Answer all the surprising and provocative "ifs" it provides, and the gates to your future will swing open before you."

Alan Morinis
Author of *Climbing Jacob's Ladder*

"One of the more interesting "quirks" of the Hebrew language is that the word for "if" and the word for "with" are the same - the word "im." In a strange way, ifs are connectors, bringing us together, together "with" others, together "with" our tradition. That is, IF we respond correctly to the ifs of life, life itself being a word with IF in the middle, as in lIFe. Here, in this book, are a multitude of ifs that forge a with. Engage, and enjoy."

Rabbi Reuven Bulka
Author of *Turning Grief Into Gratitude*

Introduction: The Pondering Jew

For thousands of years, the Jewish people have been asking questions and answering them with another question. Perhaps Cain's response to G!d served as the model: "Where is Abel your brother?" "Am I my brother's keeper?" Also, the Passover Seder trains young Jewish children to ask four questions, but why stop at four?

Not all Jewish questions begin with the word, "if", but some famous ones do. Hillel the Sage famously asked a triple "if" question: "If I am not for myself, who will be for me? But if I am only for myself, who am I? If not now, when?" (Ethics of the Fathers 1:14). Hillel's rhetorical question does not beg for an answer, but the questions included in this collection do.

In modern times, Tevye the Milkman, wondered, "If I were a rich man…" Indeed, questions beginning with the word "if" lend themselves to delightful pondering.

Whether the questions in this collection are answered around the Shabbat table, the Pesach Table, or no table at all, we hope that they offer some hearty Jewish food for thought and discussion.

1. If the Mashiach (Messiah) was alive today, who do you think it might be?

2. If you could travel back in time and meet any Biblical character, who would it be?

3. If you could travel back in time and meet any Jewish person, who would it be?

4. If you could live in any Jewish era or time period, which would it be?

5. If you could invite anyone from the past to your Shabbat table for dinner, who would it be?

6. If you could invite anyone from the past to your Pesach Seder, who would it be?

7. If you could design your own synagogue, what would it look like?

8. If you had to live in any city in Israel, which would it be?

9. If you could live to be as old as Metushelach (969), would you want to live that long and why or why not?

10.   If you had the opportunity to meet Moses, would you want to and why or why not?

11.   If you could save someone's life, but it would decrease your life by ten years, would you do it?

12.   If G!d would grant you any prayer or wish, what would you pray or wish for?

13.   If G!d would grant you any trait or quality, what would you request?

14.   If you were to move to Israel, what would you need?

15.   If you were to get rid of one Jewish practice, which would you remove?

16.   If you were to add one Jewish practice, what would you add?

17.   If you were to write one Jewish book, what would it be?

18.   If you could change anything about Judaism, what would it be?

19.   If you could become an expert on one Jewish book, which would it be?

20.   If you have children (again), where would you like to send them to school, and what kind of an education would you want them to have?

21.   If you could have an ideal rebbe/rabbi, what would the rebbe/rabbi be like?

22.   If you could change one thing about the High Holidays, what would it be?

23.   If you could remove any holiday from the Jewish calendar, which one would it be?

24.   If Moses had not led the people to Canaan as the Promised Land, where would you have preferred the Promised Land to be?

25.   If you could have prevented any event in Jewish History, which would it be?

26.   If Judaism has one gift or message to the world, what do you think it is?

27.   If you were stranded on a desert Island and could bring only one Jewish food, what would you choose?

28. If you were stranded on a desert island with only one other person, a Biblical character, who would you choose?

29. If you were stranded on a desert island and could bring only one Jewish book, which would you choose?

30. If all of your best friends would move to Israel, would you go with them?

31. If you could ask G!d any question, what would you ask?

32.	If you could make one non-kosher food kosher, which would you transform?

33.	If you were to start a new kosher restaurant, what kind of restaurant would it be?

34.	If there is one underrated Jewish holiday, which do you think it is?

35.	If you could change any Shabbat law, what would it be?

36. If you had your ideal Shabbat, what would it be like?

37. If you could spend one holiday in Israel, which would you choose?

38. If you could celebrate Pesach in your ideal way, what would it be like?

39. If you could honour one Jewish person, who would that person be and how would you honour him or her?

40. If you could change anything about Jewish prayer services, what would you change?

41. If you could add a prayer to the regular prayer service, what would you add?

42. If you won a million dollars and could do anything with it, what would you do?

43. If you won a million dollars but had to give it all to tzedaka, where would you give it?

44. If you could work in any position in the Jewish community, what would you choose?

45. If your child were to marry someone non-Jewish, what would you do?

46. If someone told you that Mashiach had arrived, what would you do?

47. If Chava did not eat from the Tree of the Knowledge of Good and Evil, what would the world be like?

48. If you could add any book to the Bible, which would you add?

49.   If there was a school for prophets, would you enrol and why or why not? If the tuition were very high would you still enrol?

50.   If you could study with any Jewish teacher from the past, who would it be?

51.   If you were to work to create peace in the Middle East, which world leader would you approach first and why?

52.   If you could appoint anyone as president of Israel, who would it be?

53.   If you could make any non-Jewish person Jewish, who would you bring into the tribe?

54.   If you could speak with Moses, what would you say?

55.   If you could speak with Albert Einstein, what would you ask him?

56.   If you were G!d, what would you do?

57.   If you were threatened to be killed or convert to another religion, what would you do?

58.　If you could be any Jewish holiday, which would you be?

59.　If you could witness any historical Jewish event, which would you choose?

60.　If you could invite any Jewish comedian to your party, who would you book?

61.　If you could meet any Jewish sports celebrity, who would you choose?

62.   If you could have any Jewish musician play at your simcha (celebration), who would you choose?

63.   If you could have (/had) any rabbi be your mesader kiddushin (officiate at your wedding) who would it be?

64.   If you could cook any Jewish food easily, which would it be?

65.   If you needed to sacrifice one Jewish practice that you currently observe in order to save your life, which would you choose?

66. If you were faced with a moral dilemma, which Jewish book would you consult first?

67. If you could make a Jewish movie, what would it be?

68. If Moses and Abraham were drowning, who would you save first and why?

69. If you had to be any character in "Fiddler on the Roof", which would you choose?

70. If you could speak any Jewish language that you do not speak, which would you choose?

71.   If you could write a sequel to any Biblical story, which would it be?

72.   If you could write a sequel to any Jewish book or movie, which would it be?

73.   If you could meet any Jewish author, who would you choose?

74.   If you could make a special invention to help the Jewish people, what would you make?

75.   If you could create positive diplomatic relations between Israel and any other country, which would you choose?

76. If you could meet any Jewish scientist, who would you choose?

77. If you could witness one Biblical miracle, what would you choose?

78. If you could eat manna, what would you want it to taste like?

79. If you could be an expert on any Jewish subject, which would you choose?

80. If one by one, you had to place everyone around you right now in a Biblical story that suits them the best, when and where would you place them?

81. If you could lead any Jewish organization, which would you choose?

82. If you could spend a day with any living Jew, who would you choose?

83. If you could, in retrospect, change one thing about your Jewish upbringing, what would it be?

84. If you could give semicha (ordination) to anyone as a rabbi, who would you ordain?

85. If you could possess any object from Jewish history, what would you choose?

86. If you could say anything to the Chief Rabbis of Israel, what would you say?

87. If your father could be a famous person from Jewish history, who would you choose?

88. If your mother could be a famous person from Jewish history, who would you choose?

89.   If you could have one person from Jewish history live his or her life over again, beginning now, who would you pick?

90.   If you could choose a new Hebrew name what would it be?

91.   If you could have said one sentence to Hitler while he was alive, what would you have said?

92.   If you had to convert to a different religion, which would you choose?

93.   If you could call any living Jew for advice tonight, who would you call?

94. If you could call any person from Jewish history for advice tonight, who would it be?

95. If you could have been the author of any single Jewish book already written, which book would you like to have penned?

96. If you could eat any specific food on Shabbat, what would it be?

97. If you could go to any country to celebrate Shabbat, where would you go?

98. If you could bring back any past leader of Israel to run the country again, who would it be?

99. If you could have composed any single piece of Jewish music that already exists, which would you choose?

100. If you could convert any building in the world into a synagogue, which would you choose?

101. If you could nominate anyone as Jewish person of the year, who would you nominate and why?

102. If you could transport any modern person back into a Biblical story, who would you choose and why?

103. If you could give a gift to any single Jewish person alive today, who would it be, what would you give them, and how would you present it to them?

104. If you could decide what will be written on your gravestone, what would you have inscribed?

105. If your country had to enact one Jewish Law, what would you like it to be?

106. If you were in charge of an advertising campaign for Judaism, what would you do?

107. If you could discover an item that belonged to someone in Jewish history, whose would you like it to be and what would you like it to be?

108. If you could see only one Jewish movie ever again for the rest of your life, what film would you choose?

109. If you could read the diary of one Jewish person who you know personally, whose diary would you like to read?

110. If you could read the diary of one Jewish person who you do not know personally, whose would it be?

111. If you could do one thing that would improve relations between Jews and non-Jews, what would you do?

112. If you could do one thing that would improve relations between Jews and Palestinians, what would it be?

113. If you were to select the next Jewish astronaut, who would it be?

114. If you could pray to G!d to change one of your personality traits, what would it be?

115. If you could adopt one personality trait from any Biblical character, what would you take and from who?

116. If you could have a romance with any Biblical character, who would you choose?

117. If you could have a romance with any Jewish historical character, who would you choose?

118. If you were to initiate a new Jewish charity, what would its mission be and who would benefit from it?

119. If you were to start a new synagogue, what would you name it?

120. If you had to have fought in any historical Jewish war, which would you choose?

121. If you had to name the single most regrettable thing about Jewish history, what would you name?

122. If you could discover that something that you thought was true about Jewish history was actually false, what would you wish it to be?

123. If you could take any sitcom and make the characters Jewish, which would you change?

124. If you could leave a stone on any Jewish person's grave, who would it be?

125. If you could invite any Jew to the faculty of your university, who would you invite?

126. If you could wake up tomorrow and learn that the major newspaper headlines were about Jews, what would you want them to say?

127. If you could have an email correspondence with any Jewish person alive today, who would you like it to be?

128. If you could offer G!d any thanksgiving offering what would you bring?

129. If you could have been the architect of any building in Jewish history, which would you choose?

130.	If you could be a member of any Jewish club or association in the world, which would you choose?

131.	If you were given $5000 to spend in any Judaica store in the world, what would you buy and where would you do your shopping?

132.	If you had to die in one of Jewish history's disasters, which one would you pick?

133.	If you could ensure that your child has one Jewish experience that you have had yourself, what would you want it to be?

134.   If you could join any of the twelve tribes (for free), which would you choose?

135.   If you could have any job in the Temple, which would you choose?

136.   If you were to be buried in any place in Israel, where would it be?

137.   If you were the leader of Israel, what would be your first official act?

138.   If you were to have one piece of Jewish music softly playing in your mind for the rest of your life, what would you choose?

139. If you could pray with any other person who would it be?

140. If you could put together your dream minyan, who would it be?

141. If you had to select any Biblical object that best represents your personality, what would it be?

142. If you were to get rid of one of the Ten Commandments, which would it be?

143. If you were to add an eleventh commandment, what would it be?

144. If you could have any Biblical character cook you a meal, who would you want it to be?

145. If you could be either a prophet or a sage, which would you choose?

146. If you could have any historical Jewish figure give your hesped (eulogy), who would you want to do it?

147. If you could be either a religious leader or a political leader, which would you choose?

148. If you could choose any Biblical personality to be the animator of a game show, who would you choose?

149. If you could be the editor of any Jewish newspaper, magazine or publication, which would you pick?

150. If you could dance with any Biblical person, who would you choose?

151. If you needed a Biblical figure to hire as a babysitter, who would you choose?

152. If you had to choose your favourite book in the Bible, which would it be?

153. If you had to pick you favourite Biblical story, which would it be?

154. If you could have a meal at the home of any couple in the Bible, who would it be?

155. If you could give any Biblical character a home appliance, what would you give and to who?

156. If you were to select a food that best describes your view of Judaism, what would it be?

157. If you were to pick your most special Jewish experience, what would it be?

158. If one object best represents Judaism, what is it?

159. If you were to design a new Jewish stamp, what would it be?

160. If there were a Jewish constellation what would it be named?

161. If you had to name a Jewish spaceship, what name would you give it?

162. If you could choose a new Jewish captain for Star Trek, who would the captain be?

163. If you were asked to add Jewish content to your computer, what would you do?

164. If you were to design your ideal Jewish summer camp, what would it be like?

165. If you were to design your ideal Jewish restaurant, what would it be like?

166. If you were to design your ideal Jewish community, what would it be like?

167. If you had to choose a time in Jewish history when overall things were better than any other time, when would say it was?

168. If you had to rename your city after a Jewish person, what would you call it?

169. If you had to choose a Jewish artist to redecorate your home, who would it be?

170. If you could marry any Biblical person, who would it be?

171.   If you could marry any non-Biblical person in Jewish history, would it be?

172.   If you could design the logo for the Olympics in Israel, what would it be?

173.   If you could choose any four people in Jewish history to be your pallbearers at your funeral, who would you choose?

174.   If you had to pick your favourite Jewish hero, who would it be?

175.   If you were asked to make a purchase of a new Jewish item for your home, what would it be?

176. If you could ask King David to write you a special psalm, what kind of prayer would you ask for?

177. If you could ask Avraham Avinu (Abraham) for a blessing, what would you ask for?

178. If you could ask Moshe Rabenu (Moses) for a blessing, what would you ask for?

179. If you could ask Aharon Hacohen (Aaron) for a blessing, what would you ask for?

180. If you could ask Sarah Imenu (Sarah) for a blessing, what would you ask for?

181.   If you could ask Rachel Imenu for a blessing, what would you ask for?

182.   If you could ask Yoseph Hatzadik (Joseph) for a blessing, what would you ask for?

183.   If you could ask Groucho Marx for a blessing, what would you ask for?

184.   If you could be a member of any Jewish person's family, which family would you like to join?

185. If you had to describe the three most important qualities of a Jewish home, what would you say they are?

186. If you had to describe the three most important qualities of a Jewish life, what would you say they are?

187. If you had to choose one season of the Jewish year as the most significant, which would you choose?

188. If you could be more like one of your Jewish relatives, who would it be and why?

189. If you could have provided information to anyone in Jewish history to prevent disaster, who would you inform and what would you say?

190. If you would find out that you were the reincarnation of anyone in Jewish history, who would you like it to be?

191. If you could choose anyone from Jewish history to be your friend, who would you choose?

192. If you could ask one question to anyone in Jewish history, who would you choose and why?

193. If you could have worked for anyone in Jewish history, who would you have liked to be your boss?

194. If you could have anyone in Jewish history as your employee, who would you choose?

195. If you had to pick your favourite food at a Jewish delicatessen, what would it be?

196. If you could appoint any historical Jewish person to be president of the United States, who would you choose?

197.	If you were sent out to be a Jewish ambassador to any country in the world, where would you choose to go and why?

198.	If you could be anywhere in Jewish history for one day as someone famous from that time, where would you choose to be, when and as who?

199.	If you could do any job in Jewish history for one day what would it be?

200.	If you had to pick your least favourite Jewish movie or movie about Jews, which would it be?

201. If you could add one sentence to the Torah, what would it say?

202. If you could be the author of any Jewish quotation, what words would you like to have uttered?

203. If you could design you own tallit (prayer shawl), what would it look like?

204. If you were to leave your children any Jewish heirloom, what would it be?

205. If the Prime Minister of Israel could appear on the front cover of Time Magazine next month, what would you like the caption to say?

206. If the Chief Rabbis of Israel could appear on the front cover of Time Magazine next month, what would you like the caption to say?

207. If you had to pick your least favourite Jewish food, what would it be?

208. If you could give your parents one Jewish gift, what would it be?

209. If you were to receive an award for one Jewish accomplishment that you have done in your lifetime, for what accomplishment would you like it to be?

210. If you could give a speech to all Jews living today, what would you say?

211. If you could change one election result from the past that affected Jewish history, which one would it be?

212. If you had to name the hardest working Jewish person you know, who would it be?

213. If you could design the clothes for any person in Jewish history, who would you choose?

214. If you could travel to any country in the world to visit its Jewish sites, where would you go?

215. If you had to pick your worst Jewish experience, what would it be?

216. If you had to pick your best Jewish experience, what would it be?

217. If you had to add one Jewish action into your daily routine, what would it be?

218. If there is one actor you wish were Jewish, who would it be?

219. If there were one musician who you wish would write Jewish songs, who would it be?

220. If Jews were legally permitted tattoos, what tattoo would you get and where on your body?

221. If you had to choose the best Jewish song ever composed, which would it be?

222. If you had to choose your least favourite Jewish song, which would it be?

223. If you were to be renamed after someone from Jewish history, whose name would you want?

224. If you could accomplish one Jewish accomplishment during the rest of your life, what would it be?

225. If there were a Jewish Olympic sport, what would it be?

226. If you could get the phone number from anyone in Jewish history, whose would you like to have?

227. If you could change one thing to make life better for your own gender as a Jew, what would you change?

228. If you could change the ending of any Biblical book, which would it be?

229. If you had to sacrifice your own life for one Jewish principle, what would it be?

230. If you could memorize any Jewish book in its entirety, which book would you want it to be?

231. If there were a Jewish racehorse, what would it be called? And would you bet on it?

232. If you had to name your favourite Jewish lifecycle event, what would it be?

233. If you had to advertise a Jewish product, which would it be and what would you say?

234. If you had to name your favourite Biblical book, what would it be?

235. If you could have any Jew from the past be your therapist, who would you choose?

236. If you could sing any Jewish song beautifully and perfectly, which would you pick?

237. If you could pick any famous Jewish person as your neighbour, who would you choose?

238. If you could have written a famous Jewish song, which one would you have liked to write?

239. If you could have experienced any Jewish victory, which would you have like to experience?

240. If you were sentenced to spend the rest of your life in prison with one Jewish person you know, who would you take with you?

241. If you could add one thing to your home to make it more spiritual, what would you add?

242. If you could change one thing in your synagogue to make it more spiritual, what would you add?

243. If you could occupy the world described in any Jewish novel or movie, which would you choose?

244. If you had to choose the most important Jewish event of the twentieth century, what would it be?

245. If you could leave a time capsule the size of a
microwave oven filled only with Jewish objects to
be found centuries from now, what would you put
inside of it?

246. If you were asked to put a Jewish gimmick in a
new cereal, what would you pick?

247. If you had to predict what the most important
Jewish development of the century will be, what
would you say?

248. If you could add one Jewish thing to your city or
town or neighbourhood, what would it be?

249. If you had to pick the most important quality for Jewish leaders today, what would it be?

250. If Judaism can assist with current environmental problems, how can it help?

251. If you had to pick your favourite Jewish expression, what would it be?

252. If you could arrange for any two Jewish singers to sing a duet, which two would you pick and what song would you have them sing?

253. If you had to pick your favourite Biblical quote, what would it be?

254. If there were a new store opening in Israel, what would you like it to be?

255. If you had to pick your favourite prayer, which would it be?

256. If you could have anyone prepare you a Shabbat meal, who would you choose?

257. If you could choose any two Jewish comedians to do a shtick/routine together, who would you choose?

258. If you could choose any two Jews to dialogue together, who would you choose?

259. If you could interview any historical Jewish person, who would you choose?

260. If you could mass-produce any Jewish item, what would it be?

261. If you could have an autograph of any person in Jewish history, who would you choose?

262. If you were asked to mint a new coin to honour any person in Jewish history, who would you choose?

263. If you could have the world's largest collection of any Jewish item, what would you choose?

264. If you could prove conclusively that any person in history was Jewish, who would you choose?

265. If you could have been the hero in any Jewish war, which war would it be?

266. If you were to design a Jewish video game, what would it be?

267. If you learned that tomorrow morning you were to be permanently exiled from your country and could take just three Jewish things with you, what would they be?

268. If you could take any Jewish class or crash course, what would it be?

269. If you could in retrospect thank one Jewish teacher that taught you, who would it be and for what would you thank them?

270. If you could turn any Jewish book into a movie, which book would you choose?

271. If you could write a prequel to any Jewish book, which would it be?

272. If you were the casting director for a movie about Abraham and Sarah, who would you cast as the main characters?

273. If you were asked to cast a remake of the "Ten Commandments", who would you choose as the main characters?

274. If you could change one thing to make life easier for your children as Jews, what would you do?

275. If you could make any Jewish holiday shorter, which would it be?

276. If you could make any Jewish holiday longer, which would it be?

277. If you could be qualified to teach any Jewish course, what would you like to be able to teach?

278. If there were one Jewish food that you would like to be able to cook better, what would it be?

279. If you had to pick the biggest crisis facing Jewry today, what would it be?

280. If you could have saved one Jewish person from history from an untimely end, who would it be?

281. If you had to choose either kugel or chulent to eat for the rest of your life, which would you choose and why?

282. If a Biblical character were to play you in a film, who would you choose?

283. If there were one rabbi you wish would still be alive, who would it be?

284. If there were one thing that you would like to improve about Jewish education, what would it be?

285. If any woman in Jewish history could be president of the United States, who would you choose?

286. If you had to choose your favourite female Biblical character, who would it be?

287. If you had to choose your favourite woman in Jewish history, who would it be?

288. If you could choose any past or present musician to be your synagogue's cantor, who would you choose?

289. If you could be a cantor or a rabbi, which would you choose and why?

290. If you were a shadchan/matchmaker and could set up any two people from Jewish history on a date, who would you choose?

291. If you could add one thing to a seder plate, what would it be?

292. If Judaism is to thrive, what does it need?

293. If you could create a new Jewish holiday, what would it be?

294. If you were to make a new Jewish television show, what would it be?

295. If you were to create a new Jewish magazine or blog, what would you call it and what would it be about?

296. If you could possess any miraculous Biblical power, which would you like?

297. If you could be any famous Jewish actor, who would you like to be?

298. If you could be any famous Jewish musician, who would you like to be?

299. If you could be any famous Jewish politician, who would you choose?

300. If you could have any synagogue in the world as your synagogue, which would you choose?

301. If you could add a fifth question to the Pesach Seder, what would it be?

302. If you had to be either Tevye or Yentl, which would you choose?

303. If you were to write a note for the Kotel right now, what would it say?

304. If you were allowed to celebrate only one Jewish holiday, which would it be?

305. If you had to be one of the Marx brothers, which would you choose to be?

306. If you had to be one of the three stooges, which would it be?

307. If you could be in any Woody Allen film, which would you choose?

308. If you could have attended any Jewish wedding in history, which would you have like to have attended?

309. If you could have attended any Bar or Bat Mitzvah in history, whose would you have like to have attended?

310. If you had to be either a mohel (ritual circumcisor) or a shochet (ritual slaughterer), which would you be?

311.   If you could have a photograph of any event in Jewish history, which would you choose?

312.   If you could have a photograph of any person in Jewish history, who would you choose?

313.   If the original tablets were sold on e-bay, for how much would they sell?

314.   If the Ark of the Covenant went on auction at Sotheby's, for how much would it sell?

315.   If you were to choose between a ride on Noah's ark or King Solomon's fastest chariot, which would you pick?

316. If you could eat either the Fruit of the Tree of Life or the Tree of Knowledge of Good and Evil, which would you choose?

317. If you could experience either the giving of the Ten Commandments of the splitting of the Reed Sea, which would you choose?

318. If you could eliminate one of the Ten Plagues, which would you choose?

319. If you could add a plague to the Ten Plagues, what would you add?

320. If you were to write a Jewish play, what would be the topic?

321. If you were to design a Jewish kite, what image would you put on it?

322. If you were to invent a new Jewish superhero, what would the name be?

323. If you had to choose between no more Jewish food and only Jewish food, which would you choose?

324. If you could be the Prime Minister of Israel or the President of the United States, which would you prefer to be?

325. If you had to pick between Chanuka and Purim, which would you choose?

326. If you were asked to select the new Chief Rabbi of Israel, who would you pick?

327. If you were asked to design a new environmental ritual for Tu B'shvat, what would you suggest?

328. If you could choose that your child either be a rabbi or a doctor, which would you choose?

329. If you could design a Jewish ride at Disney World, what would it be?

330. If you could design any Jewish ritual object, what would it be?

331. If you were to design a new Jewish ritual, what would it be?

332. If we had a Third Temple, how would it affect your life?

333. If you could pray anywhere, where would you pray?

334. If you could break the world record for doing anything Jewish, what would it be?

335. If you were to name the most underrated male Biblical character, who would it be?

336. If you could give your spouse a blessing what would it be?

337. If you could do one thing to help Jewish singles meet other singles, what would it be?

338. If you could visit any synagogue, which would it be?

339. If you could visit any Jewish museum, which would it be?

340. If you could create a new Jewish museum, what would it be?

341. If you could send anyone you know to Israel, who would it be?

342. If your child converted to another religion what would you do?

343. If there something you can do to combat anti-Semitism, what is it?

344. If your country club did not allow Jews, what would you do?

345. If your child wanted to go to a yeshiva, what would you do?

346. If your best friend became increasingly religiously observant, what would you think?

347. If you could ask your father for a blessing, what would it be?

348. If you could ask your mother for a blessing, what would it be?

349. If you could bless your child with a blessing, what would it be?

350. If you had a walking disability, how would your practice of Judaism differ?

351. If you had a hearing disability, how would your practice of Judaism differ?

352. If you were to bring more joy to Judaism, what would you do?

353. If you could experience the Judaism of two generations ago, what would it be like?

354. If you could experience the Judaism of two generations from now, what would it look like?

355. If you could design any new Jewish toy what would it be?

356. If the Mashiach (Messiah) were someone in your family, who would you think it might be?

357. If the Mashiach (Messiah) was one of your friends, who do you think it might be?

358. If you had a choice between kasha (buckwheat), kugel (baked pudding), kishkas (cooked intestines), knishes (dumplings) or kneidels (soup dumpling), which would you choose?

359. If there is one Jewish stereotype that disturbs you, what is it?

360. If you could invite any living person to your Shabbat table for dinner, who would it be?

361. If you could invite any living person to your Pesach Seder, who would it be?

362. If you could learn from any living Jewish teacher, who would it be?

363. If you could watch any person praying who would it be?

364. If you were colonizing the moon, what Jewish objects would you bring?

365. If you could legislate a new Shabbat law, what would it be?

366. If Jews have one friend in the world, who is it?

367. If Jews have had one friend, who was it?

368. If you could give a raise to your local rabbi, to your local Hebrew schoolteacher, or to your local Jewish deli worker, who would you choose?

369. If you could appoint any living Jew to be the president of the United States, who would you choose?

370. If there is something that reminds you of your Bubbe(s)/Savta (grandmother), what is it?

371. If there is something that reminds you of your Zayde(s)/Saba (grandfather), what is it?

372. If one of your children could be a famous person from Jewish history, who would you choose?

373.   If you were to name the best thing about Judaism, what would it be?

374.   If you could have any living Jew call you for advice, who would you like to call you?

375.   If you could have had any person from Jewish history call you for advice, who would you have liked to call you?

376.   If you could go on a Jewish cruise anywhere, where would you like to go?

377. If you could celebrate Pesach in any country other than Israel or where you currently live, which would you choose?

378. If you could hear a dvar Torah/sermon from anyone in the world during the High Holidays, who would you choose?

379. If you could choose any historical Jewish personality to be a news anchor, who would you choose?

380. If you had to pick a new Israeli anthem, what would it be?

381. If you had to choose the holiest day of the Jewish year, which would you say it is?

382. If you had to choose one thing that Jews can improve, what would it be?

383. If you could choose any symbol to be on your synagogue's parochet (ark cover), which would you choose?

384. If Jews can make one contribution to tikkun olam (repair of the world), what is it?

385. If you could choose that your child would either be a mensch (good human being) or have a successful career, which would you choose?

386. If you could have any Jew from the past tell you a story, who would it be?

387. If you had to pick the most important Jewish teaching, what would it be?

388. If you had to pick the biggest crisis facing Israel today, what would it be?

389. If you were to name the most underrated female Biblical character, who would it be?

390. If you were to name the most underrated non-Biblical Jewish historical person, who would it be?

391. If you were to name the most underrated currently living Jewish person, who would it be?

392. If you could give your mother a blessing, what would it be?

393. If you could give your father a blessing, what would it be?

394. If you had to describe your biggest religious crisis, what would it be?

395. If you had to describe your biggest religious question, what would it be?

396. If you could be any Jew alive today, who would you choose to be?

397. If there is one thing you like about going to synagogue, what is it?

398. If there is one thing you dislike about going to synagogue, what is it?

399. If there is one thing you would like to change in your life for the coming year, what would it be?

400. If there is one thing you would like to change in your emotional life, what would it be?

401. If you had to choose between living in a city of all Jews or a city of no Jews, which would you choose?

402. If you could build your ideal Sukkah (ritual booth), what would it look like?

403. If you could have the key to any place in Israel, what would you choose?

404. If we did not blow the shofar (ram's horn) on the High Holidays, what instrument would you suggest to use?

405. If you could choose to be King Saul, King David, or King Solomon, who would you choose?

406. If you were asked to introduce a new fast day to the calendar, what would you suggest and why?

407. If you could add any letter to the Hebrew alphabet, what would it be?

408. If you had to serve in the Israeli army, how would you like to serve?

409. If you were G!d during the Shoah (Holocaust), what would you do?

410. If there were one environmental improvement you could make to Israel, what would it be?

411. If you could write a biography about any famous Jew, who would it be?

412. If you were rabbi of your community, what would you do?

413. If you had to do it all over again, would you choose to be Jewish?

414. If you could do one thing to ensure that your children's children will be Jewish, what would it be?

415. If Pharaoh had not subjugated the Jews, would we have had Passover?

416. If you had one day left to live, what would you do?

417. If your best friend needed a kidney, would you donate yours?

418. If a poor person came knocking on your door late at night, would you welcome that person in and feed that person?

419. If Adam had not blamed his wife for eating the fruit, would God still have banished him from the Garden?

420. If Adam and Eve had not eaten the Fruit of the Tree, what would the world look like?

421. If you could choose an afterlife, what would you choose?

422. If...

About the Authors

Karin Tulchinsky Cohen lives with her husband and children in Silver Springs, Maryland. She is also the author of *Creating Effective Programs for Gifted Students with Learning Disabilities*.

Rabbi Schachar Orenstein has served as a congregational rabbi in Vancouver and Montreal for many years, including at Congregation Shaar Hashomayim, the Spanish & Portuguese Congregation and Shir Chadash. He co-founded the Montreal Open Shul and can be contacted at rabbischachar@gmail.com.

www.ingramcontent.com/pod-product-compliance
Lightning Source LLC
Chambersburg PA
CBHW032254070726
47590CB00016B/2796